I0777142

Ethicarianism

(Ethicarian Diet and Life)

"There exists a greater pleasure than eating: Letting live"

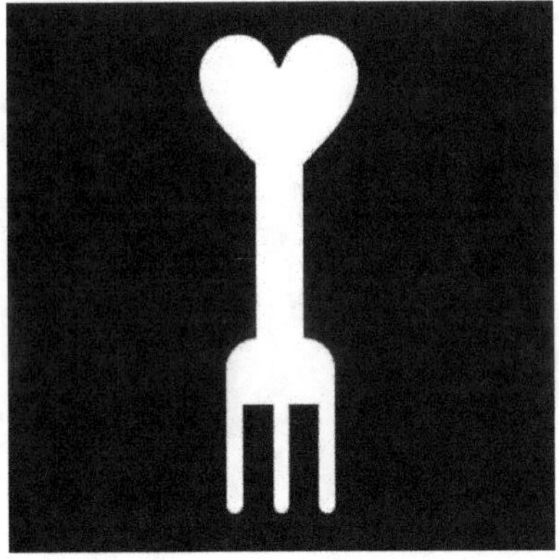

Tomás Vega Moralejo

(English translation: Cristina Sánchez Moralejo)

INDEX

FOREWORD

In the book *Ethicarian Cooking* (Bubok Publishing. Madrid, 2015) [*only in Spanish*] I made a presentation of this diet concept, apart from including a series of recipes, selected mainly thinking about making it easier to shift from meat eater to vegetable eater in its place. It also included a guide of nutrition data (composition of the main foods containing proteins, carbohydrates and fats, as well as their caloric contribution, and a look at other outstanding features, such as cholesterol), a guide of cooking times of the main foods, in the oven, boiled/cooked and in the microwave; and a guide of food additives (antioxidants such as E-300, ascorbic acid, etc.) and their safety or convenience of avoiding them.

That book, in brief, was "several books in one book", but in this one I wanted to focus on and delve into the theoretical part of this way of eating, and even of living, and I have dispensed with the three guides, as well as with the collection of recipes, although as regards the recipes, I will give indeed some ideas. The aim is to make a shorter and cheaper book, and, therefore, more accessible, and direct it to those who remain with the doubt, but at least have ever thought (if not, they would not approach such a book) about taking the step of looking beyond and realizing that their way of consuming affects other beings in a more direct way than it seems.

***

Let me treat you informally every now and then and let me start with my personal experience with reference to the eating change, as I spent 35 years eating as most western people do.

You might wonder who I am, that my personal experience would be of interest ::: well, precisely, "a nobody", so the interest may be that "anyone", with a bit of willpower, may turn to a more ethical eating.

In the early morning hours of 7 February, 2014, a documentary changed my life: Earthlings (by Shaun Monson).

How do the animals that we use and consume in different ways, namely to eat, live? Have you seriously thought about it? Have you thoroughly thought about it?

The industries which deal with animals carefully hide the reality. Paul McCartney, one of the many distinguished vegetarians (there are more than we think), says, that if slaughterhouses had glass walls, everyone would be vegetarian... and the meaning of the sentence is clear, but if those walls were transparent, the reaction would be simply to move away from slaughterhouses... "out of sight, out of mind"; and thus, most people spend their whole life blindfolded regarding animals, without knowing that their way of consuming is probably completely against their way of thinking.

Many people would not eat lamb or any other animal if they had to kill it themselves… but if we eat meat we are paying another person to kill that lamb for us. The relationship is really as direct as that.

If you watch "Earthlings" you may probably not need further explanations, but people move away from that documentary because it is "a slaughterhouse which lets us see through the walls".

I must stress that "not to see" may help you not to feel, but it doesn't avoid what really happens.

Do you want to be a part of the most horrible mistreatments and death of innocent beings? Do you want to be an accomplice to all that sadness and pain? Probably not, but then you cannot continue to bury your head in the sand, as it is (inappropriately) said ostriches do faced with what they fear and don't want to see.

But I know that the issue is not simple. The whole society seems to have come to an agreement to be insensitive to the suffering of animals, as long as a few benefit, and the rest of us consume whatever we feel like without problems of conscience.

I myself have always had sensitivity for animals, and, therefore, the question "Is eating animals consistent with my way of thinking?" had always been at the back of my mind... but I had always justified myself with the typical """it's just that we are omnivorous, also animals eat each other, it's a rule of life, we need animal proteins for a balanced diet, etc."". Obviously that, in turn, was refuted by the fact that there are vegans who live perfectly, even athletes.

The same procedure of claiming that: since we can eat meat, let's eat it, could justify, for example, that: since we have the ability of killing, let's kill.

So let us leave entelechies aside and let us move a step forward the superficial analysis of those thoughts or set phrases; although it is not easy, because meat tastes so good...!

Stop thinking as it set out is uncomfortable and it is a setback for the own way in which we have been taught to live, and you must give your best effort to take the step. Only by raising the possibility of becoming a vegetarian will a lot of people brand you odd and will try to make fun of you... although it should be acknowledged that animal-friendly eating is fashionable and just in the time lapse between my previous book (of which I spoke before) and this one, a number of new products which fit in as ethicarian have emerged, they are increasingly accessible and they are even increasingly accomplished as regards texture and flavor as meat substitutes.

Forgive me for the comparisons, in which, of course, certain gaps need to be bridged, but you will have heard or even thought about that thing of "I respect you being a vegan, but don't try to impose your ideas"….

Now imagine another person saying "I respect you being against racism, but don't try to impose your ideas" Doesn't it sound bad?

Not anything goes.

When the slavery of dark-skinned people was normal, the one who suggested that they were like everyone else, was not just odd, but his/her integrity was at risk just for showing such thoughts… in fact, the thing ended in war in the USA, because, clearly: the master has a slave (or more), who does everything at his whim, and being taken away from him really makes his life more difficult.

Or when it was normal for the man to be master of the woman, trying to take the power away from the master over that sexual accessory, and who did the housework, really made his life more difficult, indeed… and, clearly, the thing also ended with riots.

Unfortunately, there are many countries which are still in those struggles, but will authentic riots be necessary to finally respect animals in more developed countries? … well, let us hope we have learned something from history and be more civilized. That is what this book is about, being more civilized with animals from reason, but, clearly: taking back from certain people the power to carry out their will with respect to the lives of the animals is a setback….

Let's begin with ourselves.

Society is already changing thanks to the sum of individuals who respect animals, but the cause needs more "warriors".

Take the step.

You can begin, to encourage yourself, with documentaries such as "The Cove" (Louie Psihoyos) or "Blackfish" (Gabriela Cowperthwaite), much more lighter than "Earthlings" and even with intrigue or entertainment components, but which will also make you see certain hidden truths about what happens with the animals we consume, in these cases mainly in an entertaining way, as they deal with dolphins and orcas, but, in short, they may help to gradually open our eyes. Or with books such as "El triunfo de la compasión" *[The Triumph of Compassion]* (Jesús Mosterín), "Animales, la revolución pendiente" *["Animals, the Revolution Pending"]* (Silvia Barquero), this one itself, or others more advanced such as "Animal Liberation" (Peter Singer).

There is a sort of mental leap between that of "I don't like animals to suffer, but I have to eat" and that of "I am not going to be part of the suffering of animals, I can eat other things".

One thing is to think about something and another one to be persuaded of it.

I had already noted that with the issue of abandoned dogs. I had always thought, when seeing one: "poor thing, that puppy" (but that's it).

I automatically excused any involvement in the matter, thinking that it was not my responsibility or that "that's the way life is".

Coming to "poor thing, that puppy, I am going to help that puppy" is, indeed, a real mental leap.

This last sentence in inverted commas already seems so logical to me, that what I now find hard to understand is how my mind was content with the previous one.

The trick is in persuasion... but, how to persuade ourselves? In my case, regarding dogs, the one who succeeded in persuading me, by her insistence, was my wife (I will be grateful to her forever for that, although now it is me, at least for the moment, who has to urge her to move into ethicarianism and beyond)... and the first time we both helped an abandoned dog, it turned out that it was not so difficult... that "that's the way life was", but because we let it be that way. Together we have made life different for a few dogs, and the feeling of seeing their gratitude and seeing them getting better, and finally, finding a decent owner, is something simply wonderful, which outweighs by far the drawbacks; and which gets you hooked, as I have no longer looked at animals in trouble with indifference.

With reference to diet, and even beyond, what persuaded me was the documentary Earthlings. You will have a hard time watching it, but it will probably be the push you needed to become a vegan, a vegetarian, or, at least, an ETHICARIAN… and therefore be consistent with your sensitivity for animals.

By the way, at the time I thought it was me who had created the word "eticariano" (indeed I meant it to be a new concept)… and in 2014, when looking for it on the internet, there were no results, and I even looked for "ethicarian" and nor did I find it… but it turns out that results for this term in English do appear to me today when searching, and with a date prior to 2014. In any case, I don't mind being the creator of a neologism or not… the important thing is to pass on the message for the animals.

Personally, I considered this ethicarian diet to its full extent (that is, including meat), thinking about maintaining it over time, but once I persuaded myself of the problem for the animals and that it was not that difficult for me to change my eating habits, I couldn't stop… and a year later I completely stopped eating meat and my goal is to get even closer to veganism, for which, mind you, ethicarianism is suiting me very well as a transition stage. The first thing was to drastically reduce the consumption of all types of animals and eat just those from sustainable fishing or ecological meat (by the way, just with that my cholesterol decreased in less than a year from about 230 points, where it had been stalled for years, to less than 200… even though I continue being "hooked" to sweets. Another curious detail is that, coincidence or not, I haven't had a single cold since then, nor mouth sores; and both things bothered me every few months); then I completely abandoned mammals and soon after, birds… and I am in that stage, and I swear you that it already becomes easy for me. If an inveterate ex-carnivore like me can, "anyone" (with a bit of willpower) can.

The trick, as I say, is in persuasion; you can get it by seeing the miserable life to which animals are subjected for consumption, but, also, if you want to, try otherwise and try to visit first an animal sanctuary: there you will see that a pig or a duck are no less than a dog, that they are also sensitive, loving, funny, … that also want and deserve a decent life.

There are countries where dogs are eaten, something which doesn't even cross our mind here. In the end, the difference between some animals and others is only in our heads and we can psych ourselves up that a pig is not food, the same way we consider a dog is not food.

PS: In case you read some of my previous articles, you may find views different from the ones contained in this book… because my thinking indeed has been evolving to a better understanding and respect for animals, to the extent that some say that I appear to be more worried about animals than about people….

Of course, it doesn't mean that people who appear like this, like me, do not worry about people. In fact, the concern for animals does not appear from nowhere, but from sensitivity... which admittedly is applicable to people.

That is just it, with regard to the number of people who criticize us for being concerned for animals, while those people only think about themselves or at most about any of their relatives.

What happens is that the concern for people is so obvious, that not only does it not need us to make demonstrations, but it is regulated by law and it is supported unreservedly by society.

Imagine a case of mistreatment of a woman... and imagine that that case, to top it all off, was not punishable by law nor by society. Wouldn't you find it outrageous and even more serious?

Well, that is what happens to us with animals, we are fed up with not just injustices being committed against them, but even with their going unpunished, and the authorities and the whole of society being accomplices for looking the other way; and we have it all right here, in our country.

It is the next step in the achievement of moral rights after that of dark-skinned people, women and the different sexual orientations. One can take sides with goodness, or with those who also refused to see that it was absurd to enslave beings on the basis of their color or underestimate beings on the basis of their sex. It is also absurd to cause unnecessary suffering to beings on the basis of their species.

ETHICARIANISM

(Not so many) years ago, eating meat was something little more than for special occasions.

Things have reversed today, to the point that buying animal foodstuff is so affordable and accessible that, driven by taste, most people in developed countries feed themselves mainly with animals. The cost to our health is high, but it means a daily "holocaust" for the animals... of which we are not even aware of if we don't put our minds to it.

Not only are we eating too much meat, but with it we will be almost always consuming unhealthy substances produced by the animal itself, by the stress to which it is subjected, or harmful chemicals with which they are treated to control them better or increase production.

However, eating animals has become so normal, that it is hard to consider stop doing it. It is something already sociocultural; the meat industry and others have managed to deceive us so well, that most people think about happy pigs and chickens, when at most they get to think that the steak that they have in front of them was a live animal a little while ago.

COME ON, SERIOUSLY! WAKE UP! ... JUST IN CASE YOU'RE BEING DRIVEN SIMPLY BY THE INERTIA OF READING: STOP TO THINK! *Your consumption of animals results in abused animals and in animals being killed.* That's the way it is.

Let's see it with data. It may be better captured this way.

Let's take 2015, a year from which there are already final government data.

"ANNUAL SURVEY ON LIVESTOCK SLAUGHTER AT SLAUGHTERHOUSES IN 2015" (SPAIN):

2,333,895 bovine specimens.

9,960,176 ovine specimens.

1,210,269 caprine specimens.

45,890,524 porcine specimens.

52,908 equine specimens.

51,880,000 rabbit specimens.

736,455,000 bird specimens.

TOTAL: 847,783,050

Rounding it up a bit, 850 million animals sacrificed in just one year… and we are just speaking of meat industry data.

In 2015, rounding it up slightly, there were 46.5 million people in Spain.

That is to say, thereby it corresponds to 0.05 bovine specimens per person, 0.21 ovine specimens, 0.026 caprine specimens, 0.98 porcine specimens, 0.001 equine specimens, 1.11 rabbit specimens and 15.83 bird specimens. 18.28 animals per person.

It is clear that these data give room to numerous clarifications, beginning with the fact that they are just an average which, for example, in my case, fell far short, but since it is not easy to calculate each particular case, let's keep that figure.

Since supply and demand meet, just by stopping eating meat you will stop participating in the mistreatment and death of around 20 animals per year. Assume you are 30 years old, you give up meat now and you're going to live until 80... You will have lifted A THOUSAND animals out of that bloody production line.

Is it worth it or not?

Intensive livestock farming has prevailed and, in it, animal welfare is the least of the worries: hens and chickens locked in cages where they cannot even stretch their wings (to save space); calves immediately separated from their mothers (from which we steal the milk) and locked up in cells where they can't even turn around so that, through lack of movement, their meat is more tender... and fed with iron deficiency so that their meat is whiter; imprisoned sows so that they cannot get up and their offspring can be breastfed all the time until they are taken away from them; ducks forced to remain still and force-fed to make their liver diseased (*foie*); etcetera, etcetera, etcetera.

The mere fact of consuming animals makes us participants of that hell on earth, so, if we are sensitive persons, we cannot remain impassive:

The ethicarian diet is, basically, a diet in which the consumption of animal products is reduced (to the minimum we are capable of), and the few which are consumed are given the condition that they come from organic farming or sustainable fishing.

(Ethics is the set of moral principles that govern human behavior, and the moral norm in food should certainly be that our way of feeding ourselves does not cause unnecessary suffering to other beings)

The aim of this diet is to make it more palatable than a strict vegetarian diet (since a lot of people don't even consider it because they find it very restrictive), and more respectful than the usual one or even the traditional vegetarian one, which accepts eggs and milk... where there may still be a lot of suffering if the milk is not from organic farming (although the latter is not the ideal either) or the eggs, at least free-range ones.

It is important to point out right now that **such a diet is not more expensive than a standard diet**, as organic farming and sustainable fishing products are more expensive than the normal ones, but the first assumption is to reduce the consumption of animal products... and since the animal products (even the normal ones) are in general more expensive than the vegetable ones, the economic balance is offset or is even more in favor of ethicarianism. The ethicarian diet may well be then cheaper than a standard diet, because it is based on Vegetables, which are cheaper than Animal products… with the additional advantage that what we eat from animals will be of superior quality and flavor.

It cannot be overemphasized to mention that, in addition, we will be committing ourselves to promoting employment, since, obviously, intensive livestock farming (which has no place in this diet) proportionally employs less manpower.

We have increasing information accessible to really know what we eat and, although this proposed diet is not as perfect as the vegan one could be (it disregards all the products of animal origin), at least it can serve to reduce our impact on animals to the extent we want or we are capable of approaching veganism.

I must stop to point out, since it is possible that a vegan person might even feel offended with the considerations of the ethicarian diet, as the latter "accepts" the death of animals and a certain degree of exploitation: I admit that veganism is the moral ideal in terms of nutrition, but we must be admitted also (and this is one of the foundations of ethicarianism) that **it is better "something" than nothing** … and it is a fact that most people are completely unwilling to become a vegan and the thing has reached the point where the positions polarize and veganism is considered as something radical that provokes immediate rejection and, sadly, even discussions between the ones who consider themselves more animal-lovers than others seem to be in fashion… thus damaging the pro-animal movement as a whole. If, for example, a policeman is corrupt or a nurse is a quack, these are considered isolated cases (and they are)… but if someone considered an advocate of animals says or does something awful, people quickly use this example to speak out against the animal welfare movement as a whole. So, let's be moderate, please.

The ethicarian diet is potentially easier to be accepted by more people than the vegan and vegetarian ones, and even, as we have already said, more ethical than the latter if it doesn't have any objection to the origin of eggs and milk.

The ethicarian diet is perhaps a middle ground in the way we eat, and, with the adequate support and "advertising", it could achieve a high degree of implementation. In this respect, things are certainly not easy. Why doesn't a brand of organic eggs, for example, advertise its product by showing the reality behind the eggs from caged hens? A recurring advertising in the popular media, which showed the huge difference in the treatment received by animals in both cases, would attract more and more people to the consumption of products of animal origin where the dignified treatment matters.

The reality is that products such as eggs, milk or organic milk are more expensive and relatively few people consume them (precisely a reason that influences in their being more expensive), and the market is dominated by the companies which devote themselves simply to making money, without regard at all to the animal welfare; and a lot of companies which sell those more ethical products, also sell the "normal" ones and they are not going to shoot themselves in the foot. It is for this reason that, for the time being, the change is in our hands.

By the way, for the purpose of this diet, consuming organic vegetables is not only not necessary, but it may even be counter-productive, because organic farming is less productive and therefore, it requires a comparatively bigger tract of land than the conventional one... with the resulting environmental problems. The animals for organic meat are fed with organic vegetables, but, in addition, they live better, and that is what it is about.

Incidentally, some notes about GM products: even though transgenic plants are often sterile (not out of respect for nature, which, unfortunately, usually matters little, but to make sure that there is the need to keep on buying the product from the brand in question, not being able to reproduce it), the environmental controversy is beyond doubt, because they can compete and do away with natural varieties or cause certain imbalances, for example, for their resistance to insects. With regard to their consumption, not all the doubts have been cleared up either (there are the ones, for example, allergy-related), as it is a complex issue... but, in principle, we can be assured, because genetic manipulation (for example, for a vegetable to make thicker walls and give itself resistance to certain pests), in products and in the way it is allowed, doesn't lead to nutritional conflicts. However, it is a very good thing for them to be called into question so that precautions are taken with the handling.

Why should we have regard for animals? Out of morals, as they are beings with capacities such as suffering and others even superior to some humans, such as babies or people who, unfortunately, suffer from serious problems. Or is a dog by any chance not more sensitive and intelligent, for example, than a person with a deep degree of abnormality?

(Please do not misunderstand me... I have a daughter I adore and I would even if she had any disability. Also for me a baby comes before, but there are those who disregard animals because they say that they are less intelligent, and they don't realize that, by making this argument, they are actually leaving certain people behind animals.

There are those who judge the intelligence of animals to the extent that they are no table to understand it.)

But even without entering into complicated philosophical considerations, we can justify that regard for animals in a very simple way: throughout our whole life we seek to avoid or reduce suffering by all means; death is ultimately something inevitable, but suffering must be avoided or reduced whenever possible: and this provision should serve for any being capable of suffering it. If we do not want that for ourselves, why should we cause it to others?

If an animal has Eyes to See, a Stomach to Digest, ... From where is it deduced that their Brain is not for Thinking?

Let's imagine a person with something like a paralysis which prevented him/her from making sounds, gesturing, ... a person who, in short, could not communicate with us in a way we understood him/her, but whose mind worked well for him/herself. And let's imagine he/she had just lost a loved one and he/she was aware of it.

Failure to appreciate (because of their defects) their signs of pain, failure to hear their moans, … Does it mean that this person does not suffer?

The fact that we can only imagine the suffering of others is a problem for persuasion… and hard to imagine if we ourselves have not suffered something similar before (How to imagine the suffering of a person with migraine if we are fortunate of not having ever had a headache?).

At least "normal" people can manifest their sufferings one another in different ways, but the mere fact that we don't understand animals should not make us conclude that they are unable to feel and suffer.

In many cases, in addition, it is merely a question of paying some attention. In many cases, the signs of feeling are there, although there are those who may not notice them. A dog cannot smile, but it can wag its tail out of joy instead. Dogs are capable of grasping the joy in a person, even if he/she doesn't have a tail; refusing to see the joy in a dog, just because it cannot smile or show it in a "human" way, is a coarse excuse for not getting along.

Certain people take it to the extreme, even denying that an animal suffers when it is crying in pain… and do so as a mere excuse to go on causing damage to the animal without their conscience being affected by it.

We have a kind of shield which, in fact, is necessary as a psychological barrier to certain factors. We cannot be completely sensitive to all suffering, or we would go crazy, or our life would be hopelessly miserable. Faced with a misfortune, our mind has its protection mechanisms and, some people better than others, are capable of overcoming adversities. We lose a loved one and we overcome, life goes on.

If he/she has been educated and desensitized for it, a person may not feel anything over the death of an animal, because he/she will have psychological barriers implanted for this to happen. And just as with animals, there are people insensitive to other people.

We could go deep into difficult philosophical questions, and even doubt the "blame" of a person mentally governed by that education or desensitization when he/she commits any misdeed. But let us not go so far, **the truth is simply that one thing is that a person is not prepared to understand the suffering of an animal and another one that animals do not suffer.**

We, the ones who are able to emphasize with animals, must try to persuade the world… although it is not easy, because many of the dog lovers, for example, show a strong reluctance to consider other mammals capable of having the same sensitivity as dogs; which is actually not something sensible, since if you give a pig the opportunity, it can be as akin to a person as a dog, although its qualities and morphological limits differ slightly.

The border people place between regard for animals and for other higher mammals, is similar to the one placed to consider their family and friends more important than strangers, or their fellow citizens more important than people from a different country. Likewise, we establish links with dogs which we give no option to establish with other animals, but it doesn't mean that the latter are less sensitive... in the same way we have finally made clear that a black person is not less sensitive than our white friend. It is normal to appreciate more our friend, as he/she is a friend, but it is by no means tolerable to provoke or wish suffering to others because of their status.

Another reason to give consideration to animals (which is more selfish, and it may therefore be more important for some people, but which is also valid) has to do with our own health: intensively farmed animals (although they are made out to be happy so that we by with no remorse) are subjected to a terrible stress by which their glands secrete harmful substances which end up in the "meat", or they are given substances which are harmful to keep them or increase their production. The World Health Organization already warns us, for instance, that the overuse of antibiotics in food animals will become a serious problem for humanity because of the resistance of bacteria to them.

Many of these animals are not even allowed to meet their basic needs, such as stretching their wings or walking. If we think about it, it is intolerable, but, additionally, it stands to reason that an animal living in this state of anxiety should ultimately not stay healthy nor be healthy.

Shall we be unhappier with this ethicarian diet, because of its disadvantages, such as doing without the flavors we like? If we persuade ourselves of what eating animals means, not only will we not be unhappy with the Ethicarian or Vegan diet, but, indeed, **we will happy with ourselves, because we will be acting in accordance with what we understand as fair**; we lose some flavors but we gain others and, above all, we gain dignity.

Besides, the palate adapts and we will end up enjoying both a lentil stew and a veal stew.

By the way, the ethicarian diet does not by any means allow the consumption of offspring of animals. Eating beef, lamb or other offspring means a double evil: the sacrifice of a young animal that should be running around happily, is coupled with the separation of mothers from their offspring... something traumatic, at least for every mammal.

We continue with some guidelines for ethicarian consumption:

-Let us be clear: in order for a cow to give milk, she has had to be pregnant; and, since the destination of the milk is not her offspring, but human consumption, it is easy to draw the conclusions that it has…. That is why our choice should be vegetable milk substitutes (soya, rice, oat, almond drink, …).

Nevertheless, since milk is an ingredient of such a widespread use that many people may find it difficult to replace it, and since we must choose the least worst option, in this book we insist on organic milk as a substitute for the regular one when someone does not tolerate the vegetable ones.

Milk from organic production, then, is not the perfect thing for the purposes we are dealing with, but there are important differences between organic farming and intensive production which, if we are not able to do without milk, "let us" opt for it:

Cows have access to open air areas, they are fed with feeds and ecological fodder, the offspring are breastfed for some time [in intensive breeding mother and offspring are immediately separated], it is not allowed to give them chemical substances, except if they are for the cure of a disease (and during this time they are set aside from the consumption chain), any kind of mutilation to the animal is forbidden (an ox, by the way, is a castrated bovine), special attention is paid to the transportation and final sacrifice being done with the minimum stress for the animal, etc.

Yet, in addition, milk of an undoubtedly superior taste and quality is obtained.

*Note: It can be really difficult or impossible to find certain dairy free products or dairy products from organic farming… and the advice is not to be obsessed, because, as we say, it is better to do "something" than "nothing". If completely renouncing to non-organic milk products, such as chocolate, for example, poses a serious obstacle to follow this diet, it is better to allow oneself a deviation from the norm than completely abandoning the diet. Besides, one of the foundations of this diet is to send out the message that we want animals to be treated with dignity: if we replace the bottle of regular milk with that of organic milk, the message is clear, but if we stop consuming something containing milk chocolate, will the manufacturer become aware that we don't consume his/her product as a matter of ethical question? Well... we must not consider this issue settled, but it may be enough, in principle, to remove from the diet just the products whose main ingredient (in cheese, for example) is non-organic milk.

-Eggs, and the same for poultry meat, must be at least free-range, organic or domestic (ours or from someone we trust).

The alphanumeric code printed on the eggs indicates their origin with the first number: 0 for organic production, 1 for free-range (the birds enjoy outdoor space), 2 for birds which are on the ground, but crammed into sheds, 3 for caged birds. The next two letters of the code indicate the country of origin [ES for Spain], the next two numbers, the province of production [24 for Leon, for example], the next three ones, the municipality and the following three ones: more concrete information within the municipality which leads us to the specific farm.

-Meats, from organic farming or animals raised in freedom, or do not eat them. Remember that, in the industrial production of meat, animal welfare is the least of concerns: if an animal has to be kept still for its meat to be tender, it is done; if an animal has to be starved and deprived of iron for its meat to be whiter, it is done; if hens have to be kept in cages which are a real torture so that the production of eggs is more efficient, it is done; and the same way with every detail which improves the economy or the presence of the end product, the agony of the animal does not matter.

-Fish, from sustainable fishing (which is the one considered to be endlessly continued: overfishing is prevented, the ecosystem is respected, the capture of unwanted species is restricted, etc).

At least, in fishing **the animal will have lived freely up to the very moment of its death** (and this is a reason why some people choose no meat/yes fish), but it should be noted that aquaculture is not always sustainable or does not always care for the animal welfare, as, in many cases, animals are kept in conditions of excessive populations (and now medications and other chemical products have to be used to keep them), or others are captured in a non-sustainable manner to feed those from aquaculture.

On the other hand, there are animals (such as mussels) which do not even need a certification of sustainable fishing, or anything like it, because they generally come from practices which do not pose a problem regarding the terms provided by the ethicarian diet. Although it is not clear, it doesn't even seem that the capacity to suffer of bivalves and other animals at the bottom of the evolutionary scale is as developed as in "superior" animals ... neither is generally the way they are sacrificed particularly bloody.

This is a controversial subject, as we can be sure that mammals have the ability to feel and suffer, but as a species moves phylogenetically away from the human one, that ability to feel and suffer is less evident... but not becoming evident to us does not mean it doesn't have it.

However, one can venture that the awareness of suffering does generally decrease as we go down the steps in the evolutionary scale. Physical pain is not necessarily accompanied by emotional or even physical distress. Physical pain is a necessary factor to activate defense mechanisms in an animal, but there may be pain without suffering... and I'm not referring to dysfunctions such as masochism, although the issue of pain is complex to such an extent.

To better understand the argument that there may be pain without suffering, let us consider something as simple as taking a bath in very cold water: sooner rather than later almost our body will hurt and, nevertheless, we may even be enjoying ourselves... although the body warns us with that pain that cold is dangerous, and the pain will increase until we are forced to get out of the water. Or let us think about the case we are given an injection: we may bear the pain of the puncture without suffering, because we know it is something beneficial for us. In short, to entail suffering, pain requires consciousness of the harm and of the danger for the integrity. And it is perfectly clear, because of the similarity of the nervous systems and because of what we can observe, that the animals which are phylogenetically close to us, humans, can feel suffering, such as mammals or birds... and it is not so clear in fish or amphibians, for example, to be finally unlikely that, for instance, bivalve mollusks have evolutionarily developed or preserved a consciousness of suffering; in fact, in what would such a thing help an animal which can do virtually nothing to escape from danger?

However, as I said, we must take these disquisitions with caution. Let us say, at least, that the less evolved a being is, the less likely it is that feeding upon it poses a moral problem... until being clear that with plants and mushrooms there is certainly none, as we are sure they do not suffer because they lack a nervous system and they work in a, so to speak, "physicochemical" way (for example: the circulation of sap in a plant is no more than a series of actions of intermolecular forces. The movement of a plant towards light is due to the presence or absence in a part of the plant of a vegetal hormone inhibited by light, ...). Still, there are people who insist on contemplating that plants may feel, generally as a crude argument to be used against those who do not eat animals. Let us be a little bit rougher with another way of debunking that myth: nowadays, organs or extremities of the body may be kept "alive" separately; so let us imagine an amputated arm still "alive"... Will this arm suffer, no matter how much we stab something in it? Obviously not, despite the fact that an arm has even nerves....

We leave pain behind. Myths must be eradicated, such as that the vegetarian diet does not provide us with the proteins we need. It is based on the fact that most vegetables do not individually contain all the amino acids in considerable amounts, but this myth is part of the propaganda of the industry involved in animal production. With simple combinations such as legumes (lentils, chickpeas, peas, beans, ...) and cereals (bread, pasta, rice, ...) we obtain proteins, both complete and more easily assimilated by the body.

A varied vegetarian diet, and in a sufficient quantity, does not require any further concerns that, if anything, not the proteins, but Vitamin B12 (it is actually the only component accepted which nutritionally may not be sufficiently provided by a strict vegetarian diet)... a reason for which it seems advisable to eat eggs (remember, free-range or organic ones), or organic milk, or bivalves, ... or a supplement of that vitamin, which is obtained with bacteria.

It is also an interested myth, one of those we invent to justify not changing, the one that with a vegetarian diet not enough nutrients or energy are obtained for activities which require effort. There are, for example, several elite athletes who are even vegans (you can find examples in the internet), but we only have to pay attention to some examples to see how far away this statement is from reality (values for portions of 100 grams, in order energy [kilocalories] / proteins [grams] / fats [grams] / carbohydrates [grams]):

*Pork loin: 311/16/27/1

*Chicken breast: 145/22/6/0

*Hake: 64/12/2/0

*Egg: 162/13/12/1

*Chickpeas: 341/21/5/44

*Pasta: 359/13/2/71

*Toasted almond: 621/23/53/7

There are vegetables which win the match against animals in nutrients and energy… and, incidentally, that way, another myth falls, which some let out according to their needs: vegetarianism makes you thinner.

The aim is to make good combinations, because an unhealthy 100% vegetable diet may also be made.

It is curious how easy it is to accept the lie that the vegetarian diet is insufficient, and the objections raised to accepting the truth all nutritionists say, that too much meat is consumed. **It is an example of cognitive dissonance.**

We people tend to belief simply what is best for our comfort, but numbers don't lie.

In vegetables, there is variety for everything; anyone who wishes to justify eating a lot of animals because of any deficiency in vegetables, is deceiving him/herself or he/she is simply little or badly informed.

I refer you to the section about proteins of this same book for more information, and, linked to it, we will see the different types of diets with mindfulness (by the way, mushrooms are not vegetables, but for reasons of simplifications they tend to be considered as such in a diet and that is what I do in this book):

-(Traditional) Vegetarianism, also called (to make it clearer) ovo-lacto vegetarianism: apart from vegetables, it allows eggs and milk (and their derivatives).

-Pescetarianism: ovo-lacto vegetarianism which adds fish and seafood to the diet.

-Chicken-pescetarianism: pescetarianism with the addition of poultry meat; it just dispenses with mammals.

-Flexitarianism: vegetarianism which allows pushing the boundaries in some cases, for example, when dining out.

-Veganism: similar to what a strict vegetarianism would be like, but which dispenses with every food of animal origin, even honey, for example. Raw veganism does not even cook the food.

All these approaches to nourishment, except for veganism, may involve great animal suffering… let us not forget that one of the most insensitive industries towards animals is precisely that of the production of eggs in cages, as they keep the hens in ridiculously reduced spaces and in which the poor hens cannot meet almost any of their basic needs, such as flapping, digging into the earth or the mere fact of moving away to lay an egg calmly.

But all these approaches to nourishment may have their ethicarian correspondence, such as "ethical vegetarianism", in which, apart from vegetables, eggs and milk are consumed, but just in the case of free-range eggs and organic milk.

As it would be incongruous to adopt a diet like this and not taking into account other ways of animal abuse, we must:

-**Inform ourselves generally.** We must take into account that our way of eating has repercussions up to where the products come from, and we must learn to look beyond the obvious:

purchasing something as simple as some cookies may seem very innocent, but we can take a look at their ingredients and ask ourselves if what they contain is ethical. For example, the use of palm oil is very common (which, in addition, is one of the worst for health, and even worse if it is palm kernel, which it is then hydrogenated), and it turns out that palm plantations are wreaking havoc on tropical forests and they are condemning many species, such as orangutans, to extinction. We must refuse to consume palm oil, unless it has a certificate of sustainability.

Or it is possible that we are even favoring the exploitation of people. Indeed, it should be noted that by protecting nature we must not forget people: when thinking, for instance, about the protection of a particular species in a particular place, one tends to forget that in that place there are also often people who may not have a life as good as ours; and asking someone who suffers from hunger and other needs not to cut trees or not to kill certain animals to survive is nonsense. We must also think about the people's welfare. Everything is related. And the good thing is that the protection of nature itself may be a source of profits. The basis is to get things well done and in balance... I have in mind, for example, the amount of roads being made, and the fact that a few are absolutely unnecessary or they pass through inappropriate places, implying waste of money and making up a sort of Berlin walls which many animals need to cross and they turn into death traps.

-Adopt instead of buying, or, in any case, treat our pets right and meet their needs (including space, of course). We must never give pets as presents.

-Avoid clothing produced from animal skins. This is very simple and the fur sector is one of the bloodiest with animals, so do not forget to make sure not to wear furs.

-(We must) not attend shows with animals. Animals do not want to act, it is not in their nature; let us leave them in peace. Kids do not need to see a confined animal making "funny" things to become fond of it, a Walt Disney movie may be enough (and I am not saying it as a joke, as I bet he even deserves a posthumous Nobel Peace Prize for all the sensitivity towards animals which his creations and his legacy transmit).

-(We must) not purchase products tested on animals. You may learn about brands free from suffering on websites such as "Cruelty Free". With regard to medical research with animals, we can do little, and in some cases the benefit obtained seems to exceed the suffering it causes… **but the trend should be to replace practices on animals with others such as, stem cells. There is a lot of excess as well and we should at least show our rejection to abusive,** repetitive (practical trainings of students, for example) or unnecessary practices (which are many more than we think, as experiments are made, as stupid as separating a monkey offspring and its mother, just to demonstrate and document that, logically, they suffer as a result). In addition, all these experiments in animals must be then made in humans as well and many of them might be done directly in humans, as, in fact, there are usually volunteers.

-(We must) not eat anything that comes from jobs in which people are exploited, a type of production, besides, clearly related to damages to animals and the environment in general.

-Support environmental associations, such as Greenpeace, PETA or WWF; or to the PACMA party.

-Act. It can be as simple as signing petitions on social networks or writing to a company asking to have vegan hamburgers as an option or to stop marketing some animal product. Let it be known and let it be noticed that we are there, and that animals matter. This, for example, is the way things are achieved, such as the fact that in August 2014 the largest food company in the world announced a commitment made with an NGO for animal welfare to impose some improvements in the treatment of animals on its supplying farms... imperfect, yet improvements, after all. That is the way to make progress, small step by small step.

-Give consciousness-raising as a present: Books or documentaries, or products sold by environmental associations. This way, in addition to the gift which can serve to raise awareness, we are helping people who promote environmentalism.

- ....

We shall continue with some doubts that might arise when becoming an ethicarian, as, curiously, our friends and family will suddenly pay a lot of attention to the way we eat and they will be attentive to the slightest slip to throw it in our face… maybe to feel better about themselves this way, because deep inside they share that killing animals, even indirectly, is not right.

Some may throw in the face as well that we also kill bugs just by walking… and in this respect I am going to transcribe a kind of a joke which I read on the internet and of which I cannot give the authorship because I do not know it:

"I thought about becoming a vegan, but even so I would go on stepping on bugs by accident. Therefore, the solution, since I cannot be perfect, is to cut the throat of chickens, pigs, cows, … apart from stepping on bugs, logically".

Irony is understood.

What to do if we go to a restaurant or we are invited to a meal? What about hunting? And plagues? How do we feed our pets? What do we do in our business if we work with products from animals or even with animals? …?

Obviously, nothing is simply black and white… and controversies also arise with this diet.

The ethicarian diet hopes to be something more or less easy to implement. It is not perfect, but **it is always best to eat less meat and that it comes from animals with a more-or-less dignified life, than not to do anything because strict vegetarianism seems impossible to us.** Accordingly, we must answer these and other questions that may arise.

Can we feed our pets in a balanced way without resorting to feedstuffs containing animals? Well, it may not be easy, because vegan feedstuffs are neither cheap nor accessible… but it is not a priority, because feedstuffs for animals generally use the leftovers from the production for people, it is not that animals are sacrificed to feed our pets.

Is hunting the equivalent to sustainable fishing in non-aquatic animals? Hunting is not a sport (a name given to embellish things somewhat and secure subsidies), it is to go out to kill animals... however, it could be accepted that, if it is well done, it would not necessarily be worse than the slaughter of farm animals. Nevertheless, hunting is a violent activity which is too often associated, among other things, with mistreatment of dogs (to hunters, all too often, a dog is nothing more than a tool), leaving animals injured or excessive killings or the killing of non-hunting species.

Regarding plagues or animals which mean a danger for us, we can and must certainly defend ourselves... but we have to find the way to defend ourselves which causes less suffering or damages to third parties; and the first thing is to ask oneself if we really have to defend ourselves or it is enough to let it pass: for example, there are those who take the genuine trouble to kill little birds because they eat the cherries from their trees, and then take a single bucket of them.

Do we stop using products from animals in our business, if they are needed? Maybe we will only ensure to harm ourselves, because those who consume that would go to another place and that's it. Maybe the most that we can do in our jobs is to try to raise awareness and, if possible, to offer ethicarian products as well....

If we live with a person who does not want to follow our diet, can we eat, for example, the chickpeas from a stew which has beef as well? Can we even eat the beef if by not doing so we would end up having to throw it away? **The important thing is that the way we eat does not "pull" the food chain in such a way that it has an impact on animals**... if the one who is with us was going to eat that beef anyway, in no way does it affect that we eat the chickpeas on the side; and given the circumstances that if we don't eat it ourselves it should be thrown away... it would mean then, on top of that, a death in vain. It is one of those occasions which we should not use as an excuse to eat meat, but it is up to each one to take the exceptional decision to eat it.

What about using animals to work? Referring, for example, to horses and other animals which are already domesticated species, and not to shows or other uses with animals which should be free.

Domesticated species could hardly now survive without our intervention... and before going on: it is not valid to state that if farm animals stop being consumed or used, they will become extinct (an argument often used also to justify bullfighting), as there are already people who have these animals as pets, and, besides, who would want to be born to suffer until death?   / Let us continue: the boundary between worthy and unworthy treatment is blurred, but there may be nothing wrong in an animal contributing to a work (we also have to work), as we provide that animal with food, safety and shelter... and I say that there may be nothing wrong as long as that animal has also its space for enjoyment, its hours of rest, it is not forced when it is tired, it has company, etc.

And, as for the first question raised, which probably represents the biggest complication of such a diet once we have become accustomed to it... with friends it is as simple as previously explaining to them and, if they are real friends, they will have no problem cooking something for us with which they respect our diet. And with regard to eating in restaurants, many of them already have ethicarian options; in those they don't, it is good to let them know our way of eating... let it be known that we are there to be taken into account; and it would be rare for a restaurant not to have a way to adapt a dish to our way of eating; if they refuse, the restaurant is not worth it....

And **in all cases of controversy, a golden rule: to be firm, but not to argue nor be annoying.**

The part of the "message" is important, it should be visible that our decision is serious, that it is possible: in public, it is the worst moment we can choose to make an exception to our diet, because any slip will be used against us and against that for which we stand up.

It is fine to explain our diet and the reason for it if we are given a non-forced opportunity, because we are the example and it is fine if we encourage someone else to follow it, but you can't get blood from a stone and getting angry or becoming annoying with someone who does not easily understand can only serve likewise to put the diet away, as well as to consider us misfits or something like that, or wasting time arguing anyway. We will find people who may even make fun of us, cases where that of "foolish words fall on deaf ears" it to be applied; and we will have to give many explanations and listen to many "illogical" apologies to try to dismantle our diet and justify the traditional one... such as -that animals from organic farming are well treated "is what they say"- to say it is a fraud, but it is only one more example that people is ready to believe anything which supports their diet and none which questions it; well, with that same reasoning, they could start doubting if mineral water actually comes from a spring or from an irrigation ditch, or from any other thing. Or they will tell us that giving up eating meat is too drastic, but it is death that is drastic... and on our part there will be a bit less; because, indeed, in addition to the message we will be directly reducing the suffering in the world.

Another typical argument to justify eating meat is made saying that "that's the way life is, lions eat gazelles as well and, is the lion evil because of that?".

It is easy to succumb to that sophistry, but, if we analyze it better, it falls down: The lion needs to eat meet to survive, we do not; and, why do we compare ourselves to the lion with its diet and not with any other of its habits, such as sleeping in the open air?

*Note: I expect all the arguments to make it clear that veganism is possible and advisable: because there is only one reason to eat animals, and that is the flavor... and there is only one reason why they want to make us believe that there are others, and that is money. But I don't forget that the ethicarian diet I propose as an alternative, in order to make it more accessible, allows meat… however, we already know: with conditions. We are persons, not carnivorous animals, and, even if we decide to eat meat, we can do it in a more civilized way than the prevailing one. What is done to animals for consumption in general is horrible.

The ethicarian diet has room for improvement, and we can take it as far as we can, up to getting into veganism.

By the way, we will surely receive good news for the palate in a near future: in August 2013, the first laboratory hamburger was presented, obtained from a culture of stem cells. For the time being it was something very expensive and not entirely satisfactory, but it looks promising, and synthetic milk is also foreseeable. In fact, such scientific advances actually seem to be the greatest hope for animals, as the people who refuse to stop eating animals will be still a lot.

Let me continue saying that I think that environmentalism lacks moderation. One often wants to put the cart before the horse and for that reason many environmentalists are labelled as radical.

For example: environmentalists call for the abolition of all forms of bullfighting in Spain, and if a politician talked about banning the "Toro de la Vega" and not "Bullfights" (because if he talked about banning "bullfights" he would probably be ensuring not to be elected and then he wouldn't even be able to implement the rest of his program and, what would be the point?), the environmentalists, instead of supporting the proposal, they went on the attack, criticizing him with an "all or nothing", for the benefit of the one who had opted for the nothing and who had been silent.... and with these radicalisms no big party is encouraged either to go for the vote of animal lovers.

Paradoxically, a great disservice is being done to animals by asking the most for them, because bullfighting (and the same is true for other matters such as hunting or speciesism [discrimination based on species differentiation] in general) nowadays is simply impossible to abolish at a stroke, because there are many interests in it and, unfortunately, a lot of people supporting it and defending it with money and power. Nevertheless, the "Toro de la Vega" did already give enough rise to controversy so as to ban it, and the abolition was achieved by insisting on that particular case.

The problem to go further is that environmentalism lacks organization, we even have animalists against animalists. Hunters, for example, are not even the 1% of the Spanish population, but their corporate spirit makes hunting untouchable. The percentage of people against animal abuse is certainly overwhelmingly greater, but there are no results without organization... hence the importance of being informed and being active, supporting those who already have a certain infrastructure, such as the major environmental associations.

Environmentalism will achieve better results once it becomes more intelligent than visceral. It should also be taken into consideration that, generally, things are not obtained with glorious actions of a hero who changes the world during the length of a film... advances, in practice, often carry boring processes. We should think about how politics works and the world itself, and we should think about not wanting to win the war directly, without its battles.

(Reflection)

Think about animals for a while.

Put yourself mentally in their shoes.

Think about how they "Live" while they wait for death to be eaten afterwards.

It is hell on earth.

Do you really want to be part of that?

Nearly all evils are a question of ego, because of people who look after their own interests and welfare, regardless of anything else... or who, at most, keep up appearances with those who are part of that welfare and those particular interests, which, in essence, is also something selfish.

Racism and sexism are already more or less overcome in developed countries, but we know how much effort it has taken to make progress with those issues and it seems to happen always the same when something which goes against the established power is questioned:

First of all, that truth is ignored, then it is made fun of, later, a violent opposition is generated (apartheid, for instance) and finally, it is accepted as something unquestionable... and this should also be the case with speciesism.

I will go back to the documentary "Earthlings" to take it as a reference, and forgive me for repeating myself about some details.

"Earthlings" is divided into five areas-ways in which we make use of animals: Pets, Food, Clothing, Entertainment and Science. Each area is full of horrifying images; some of them from relatively isolated cases against which not enough is being done to stop them happening, but, unfortunately, most of them are from usual practices... some of them from non-westernized countries, but from which we import things or "we go" there to do the misdeeds with impunity.

-With pets, the problem is that anyone (whether responsible or not) can own an animal, and the fact of being a business lends itself to improper practices. By purchasing pets in shops, we are probably participating in the fact that somewhere there are mothers enclosed, whose life is reduced to simple breeding machines... and certainly we will be participating in perpetuating the fact of having pets enclosed in the small spaces of the shops. The option is to purchase directly from decent breeders or, better: adopt, so that we will be helping really needy animals.

-With animals as food, the problem is that the current meat consumption per person is too high, which, together with overpopulation, makes the industry work also looking for meat overproduction (and eggs and milk), subjecting animals to miserable living conditions and sacrificing them in an unnecessarily cruel way... because it is cheaper to do it this way.

We eat meat and other things in ways that usually do not make us even think about the animal, and least of all about how that animal lived and died. If we knew, or if we had to take care of it ourselves, we would find it intolerable and we would not want to be involved... but the way the industry is set up is one of those blindfolds that society puts us to keep on agreeing to and even promoting things which are not right.

Meat production "needs" and so on are such that they have become an environmental problem of huge proportions: the area of land dedicated to the cultivation to feed the animals from which we eat is greater than the one dedicated directly to our food; in the USA, for instance, the cattle eat as much grain as the one necessary to feed five times its human population, and it is estimated that about 15 Kgs of grain and 15,000 liters of water are necessary to obtain 1 Kg of meat. Other sources mention that 9 Kgs of vegetable protein are necessary to produce 0.5 Kgs of animal protein; or that, if Americans reduced by 10% their meat consumption per year, 12 million tons of grain would be available for human consumption, enough to feed 60 million people.

It is clear: an animal is not simply meat and many resources are necessary to develop the latter... In terms of food, meat is absolutely inefficient.

This inefficiency in meat production has impacts therefore on hunger in the world, but also on deforestation and pollution from waste disposal. Some examples:

A farm of 2000 pigs produces 27 tons of manure and 32 tons of urine per week. In Spain alone, around 40 million pigs are slaughtered... that is a lot of shit to get rid of.

In the USA farm animals produce ten times more excrement than humans.

Each cow produces per day, as a by-product of digestion, a volume of around 200 liters of methane gas. There are 1500 million cows in the world, which pollute more than the whole transport sector, because methane is far worse than carbon dioxide in terms of greenhouse effect which is raising the temperature of the Earth. Than warming is already defrosting the Arctic, which in turn keeps a lot of methane that, in case of being released, would further increase (perhaps sharply) the global warming. If this is the case and the average temperature rises "just" about 6 degrees, it would cause a mass extinction which would probably leave us nothing to eat and the chain would end up in wars and devastation.

This is not science fiction.

...and I was talking about domestic animals: our voracity is driving many wild species directly to extinction with no need of warming.

-As for clothing, we know that much of it comes from developing countries, where, if people are barely respected, it is no wonder that nightmare scenarios happen, such as the skinning of live animals; on the other hand, in developed countries, the conditions in which animals are kept and sacrificed, from which skins are obtained, are not decent either.

-Entertainment is probably the most absurd case of animal use, as the suffering to which they are subjected is completely unnecessary. We have the prisons which are the dolphinariums and zoos in general. We have, for example, Spain with its "National Shame": bullfighting, certainly with implications beyond the sad spectacle, as it trivializes violence, and which, on top of that, they want us to pass off as culture [so as to subsidize it with everyone's money]. Also rodeos in the USA, for example, as it is not that they have such fierce bulls, but they shake the way they do because their genitals are tightened with a rope. And let us not forget circuses (and even with some animals used in films), which use animals in a bad way, whom they have taught with blows and thumps.

-Finally, the use of animals in scientific research has probably served in some cases to save lives (yes, also those of other animals), but there is also a lot of bizarre tests which have no use other than causing suffering, because, in many cases, it is known in advance that they will be useless, as they won't contribute to significant advances or they will have to be repeated on humans all the same, because, logically, an animal is not exactly the same as a person. Moreover, in many cases, experiments already done are just reproduced for trainee students, or they are used as a kind of alibi to defend the use of a product intended for marketing.

In my remarks with reference to "Earthlings" I have softened the message of the documentary. It must be admitted that this is, for each consideration, more "radical" than what I am implying with my remarks.

I have softened it intentionally, because, I have already said, I know that positions considered "extreme" (actually even if they are not) play a dirty trick on environmentalism:

Let us imagine a graduation from 1 to 10 with regard to protective measures for a species, for example, where 1 is that it is not respected at all and 10 is that it is considered in line with people. Well then, a fully aware environmentalist often immediately asks for a 10 degree of protection... and this way he/she will probably only succeed in not even being listened to, being ignored or ridiculed, as we said at the beginning about the phases.

There are no shortcuts... if the abolition of slavery and gender equality took hundreds of years (and there are still rough edges to be smoothed off), the respect for animals is still in its early stages and one should go step by step.

Nevertheless, on the other hand, it is good that also those "extremes" are "shown to us" so that those who already have some awareness gradually adopt intermediate positions. This is why we must let us be affected by "Earthlings".

As an aside, I would like to make a reflection: we are now more than 7,000 million people on Earth. The population has doubled in less than 50 years. It is evident that the more people, the greater the acceleration of population growth… and it is evident that we are doomed to disaster, because, in addition, we are historically very slow in changing. Pay attention even to what a perspective: in 1950, there were 2,500 million people, and 7,400 million people in 2016; assuming that in 1950 90% of the population was disrespectful with the environment and currently just 30%, we would now still have as many disrespectful people as then… and I have surely been generous with the percentages.

In the light of this scenario, there are two ways to take it: the easy one is to deny climate change (not necessarily "global warming", because it will affect in different ways, in different places and at different times) and so on, and to continue acting irresponsibly or even in an uncontrolled way ("as well be hanged for a sheep as for a lamb").

The other way to take it is to keep a thread of hope and try to make life more dignified on Earth while it lasts… at least so that something remains.

It looks very bad if things do not change much: strong actions would be needed…. But we must not let ourselves be discouraged. Or, don't we fight, for instance, the disease, even knowing that we will eventually die? While there is life, there is hope, and we must make life as better as possible. If thousands of beings die in a disaster, there is no giving up: we must make the effort for the ones remaining.

We all know (or there it is, on the internet, for instance, to be better informed) how to reduce our damage to the environment... now we need to apply it. We need to be soaked with information which opens our consciousness, such as that brought by those documentaries and books I have mentioned.

Closing our eyes to reality may spare us certain sufferings, but when we open our eyes and we do something about it, the reward is greater than the suffering.

Sometimes it is discouraging to "see", but it is necessary. Perpetual happiness is a utopia; no matter how much we hide, we won't be happy forever... so let us open our eyes and let us give ourselves moments of happiness by living according to what consciousness dictates to us.

A further point: as regards religions, in general obsessed with human superiority (literally, since they also tend to be male chauvinist) which has its effects against animals. I think the world would be better without religions, but I may well be wrong and the world could be better with religions... but with religions which really promoted respect in all its forms, ahead of the interests or ideas of those who handle them to manipulate the masses.

Concerning the issue here, focus on the difference: Jews, for example, have the idea that animals must be fully aware when they are bled to death and they must be sacrificed looking eastward (Would you believe it!), while an appeal by the Dalai Lama made the consumption and use of animal skins plummet among Buddhists, and many of them even burned them, even though they could have obtained with them the salary of months of work.

Religious leaders can avoid, at the stroke of a pen, a lot of suffering... let us see if they apply themselves.

Continuing with the reference of "Earthlings", I give you the "Solutions" (and I complement in brackets) to the issues it addresses:

-Pets: Don't buy, adopt. Sterilize our pets.

(And take good care of them, and keep them in suitable places, needless to say. In order to sell them, they should be kept in suitable places... with enough space and decent conditions, and in order to buy them, serious psychological tests should be passed)

-Food: Go vegan [that is, avoid any product of animal origin; including, for example, honey].

(This book is mainly devoted to this aspect, so there is not much I can add to this point. The conditions in which the animals intended for human consumption live and are sacrificed, are subject to legislation in the European Union, seeking to reduce the suffering, but there is still much room for improvement... and anyone can do their bit with the ethicarian diet)

-Clothing: Avoid clothes made of animal skins.

(As simple as that. Animal skins are a whim which causes a lot of suffering. And do not say either to those wearing fur coats that they look handsome or elegant ;-))

-Entertainment: Refuse to participate in, and, therefore, refuse to support, entertainments with animals, including circuses, zoos, etc..

(The multiple mistreatments to bulls in our country [Why do people in Spain have it out for this animal?], for instance, are not art, no matter how much they insist on giving it an honorable attribute... because, by the same token, some killers also kill with a lot of "art" .... As regards zoos, the issue has double standard, because they can (should) also play a role in the preservation of some species and in the training of children's empathy towards animals; but, at least, we should not visit exhibitions with insufficient space or in bad conditions and we should reject the area of the zoos where they perform shows with animals)

-Science: Don't buy products tested on animals. Don't support research which uses animals.

(Some cosmetic brands, for instance, indicate that they don't use animals in their research: those are the ones we like. As regards research with animals, it is a controversial issue, but at least we must signal our rejection to the excesses or not strictly necessary practices. Take a look at the "Cruelty Free" list and others to know about the "cruelty-free" companies)

Needless to say either, that you may make donations to organizations such as Greenpeace, PETA, WWF or PACMA, so that they can put more pressure.

If we don't consume (in the broadest sense of the word) pets, clothing, entertainment or products in general which imply different ways of animal mistreatment, those products will stop having an economic value and this way animals will stop being used.

Act as if what you do makes the difference... and this way, with the help of many people, at the end the difference will be made.

I come to the end and I want to highlight the book **"Animal Liberation", by Peter Singer**, most probably the definitive book about antispecism, as his arguments are irrefutable.

It is an absolutely recommendable book to Delve into what has been addressed in this one. It has hard parts, but in general it reads well... it doesn't "back you out" as much as the documentary "Earthlings" may do, so I am not going to make an extensive commentary about it: READ IT.

And I don't want to fail to transcribe two great quotes by two great thinkers, who, a long time ago, stuck up for animals, plus a couple of phrases by two authentic, modern "Jesus Christs":

Jeremy Bentham (1748-1832, Great Britain):

"Is there any reason why we should be suffered to torment animals? Not any that I can see... The day has been in which the greater part of the species, under the denomination of slaves, have been treated upon the same footing as the inferior races of animals are still. The day may come, when the rest of the animal creation may acquire those rights which never could have been withholden from them but by the hand of tyranny. The French have already discovered that the blackness of the skin is no reason why a human being should be abandoned without redress to the caprice of a tormentor. It may come one day to be recognized, that the number of the legs, the villosity of the skin, or the termination of the *os sacrum*, are reasons equally insufficient for abandoning a sensitive being to the same fate…. A full-grown horse or dog is beyond comparison a more rational, as well as a more conversable animal, than an infant of a day, or a week, or even a month, old. But the question is not, Can they *reason*? nor, Can they *talk*? but, Can they *suffer*?"

Arthur Schopenhauer (1788- 1860, Germany):

"Compassion with animals is intimately associated with goodness of character, and it may be confidently asserted that he who is cruel to animals cannot be a good man. Boundless compassion for all living beings is the surest and most certain guarantee of pure moral conduct"

Mahatma Gandhi (1869-1948, India)

"The greatness of a nation can be judged by the way its animals are treated"

Martin Luther King (1929-1968, United States)

"Even if I knew that tomorrow the world would go to pieces, I would still plant my apple tree" *(This one expresses very well the idea of "active resignation" to which I refer later)*

To conclude... Have you heard of "The Sixth Extinction"? There have apparently been five great extinctions throughout the history of our planet, for example, due to climate changes or the well-known collision of a great meteorite with the Earth... and we are already living the sixth mass extinction of land creatures, and this is directly our fault.

Some might think, And, why should this extinction be worse than the others? But, don't we consider a murder to be worse than a natural death?

It is estimated that tens of thousands of species become extinct every year, some of which we have not even got to know; each one of them is something unrecoverable and deeply sad that it disappears, and when we think about that picture, about the unrestrained growth of the human population, in which each year tens of thousands of dogs are abandoned in Spain alone, in which 600 million chickens are sacrificed every year, also in our country alone, etc..., it is easy to become discouraged and even disconsolate.

The fact of helping a few dogs or not eating meat becomes small, we feel often depressed when thinking that every second that passes by millions of animals are suffering without it being possible for us to do anything....

And it is not even that there is a kind of collusion against animals, actually, it is even worse: there they are, the wars, the enforced prostitution and many other terrible things without needing to leave the human species... and in some countries they take place with as much impunity as it does in ours with animals.

Religions try to impose their ideas, which are not even better than the ones offered by philosophy without imposition; and, in both cases, we have options of thought, but not certainties... Even science does not give answers to some major questions about life.

Only one thing comes to my mind to cope with this devastating picture about which I talk in the previous paragraphs, and it is not the extinction of the human race as some radicals propose: we humans can be the worst, but also the best.

What occurs to me is something like an **"active resignation"**. Our capacity is limited, we are not gods, therefore it makes no sense to martyr ourselves for what we cannot intervene on, because, with discouragement, not only do we fail to solve the problems, but we are also at a loss and we don't involve ourselves in alleviating them. Thus, **so far, the part of resignation: we cannot cope with everything. But we do need to be <u>active</u> with what we can:** do not waste paper (which is often underrated, but it is trees which give life) or other resources, help a dog which we find abandoned, eat in an ethicarian or vegan way, cooperate with environmental associations, do not buy products tested on animals, do not wear fur, do not go to shows with animals, participate in campaigns (even if it is just with signatures on the internet) against different ways of speciesism, etc.

Even in doing so, we must be careful not to obsess ourselves: no matter how many things we do, it may always seem that we could still do more. But there is no other way, because we wouldn't be happy acting in a manner contrary to our principles. If we don't wear furs, for instance, we can already be sure of not being involved in that part of animal exploitation, and with the other issues we must equally seek the level in which we feel comfortable... and let's live.

IDEAS TO MAKE THE CHANGE

The ethicarian diet allows cooking basically the same thing as the traditional one, as we have at our disposal almost everything in its environmentally-friendly way or similar, but we must reduce the consumption of animals to a minimum and it is possible to feed ourselves without eating products of animal origin, even without sacrificing the texture of the meat and the good flavor (something we would miss, especially at the beginning). Moreover, our palate gets accustomed to the way we eat and we will come to enjoy vegetable dishes as much as we did with those of animals... and with better digestions, better health and better awareness.

As the ethicarian diet is probably a transition towards ethical vegetarianism or towards veganism, or even to be able to stay in it without giving in, many people will find it easier if they can eat more or less the same way they did, but without affecting the animals.

Eating hamburgers, meatballs, sausages, steaks, etc., is still possible just with vegetables, not in vain a good part of the flavor of meats is given by the spices and other condiments added to them.

The change means that at the beginning we might not even know sometimes what to eat, and it has an added problem, which is the present-day hurry, but do not forget many of the more elaborate meals can be frozen so that they can be fast food when you need it.

The first idea is to let your imagination run wild and not no forget to experiment. Vary the proportions of ingredients, change replace some of them with others, …. The important thing is that you end up enjoying eating.

Try texturized soya as a substitute for meat. It is very versatile. This soya is hydrated and it is given the same flavor with the same volume of broth as the latter.

Chickpeas are also very versatile in vegetarian cuisine. Their flour, with water, may be used as an egg substitute in a potato omelette. We can mash them cooked and make meatballs with them… or we can eat them in a simple stir-fry with garlic and oil and in many other ways.

You can cook seaweed, such as Kombu, which is one of the softest, to give fish flavor with it, for instance, to texturized soya.

There are more and more ethicarian options to eat fast (pre-cooked rise, pre-fried onion, crab sticks from sustainable fishing, mayonnaise with free-range eggs, dehydrated mushrooms and vegetables, etc., etc.,) do not fail to devote some time to look closely at the shelves of the supermarkets and shops, to know what you have at hand and to have a base for ideas. You may always order the less common ingredients online if you don't find them near home.

Remember that tempura flour is a great vegan substitute for eggs, for batter.

Try vegetable milks; there are those of soya (that which has also calcium is maybe the closest to regular milk), almonds, oat, rice, coconut, …. You will probably like some of them, or all of them, and, with cocoa or coffee, you will hardly tell some of them apart from authentic milks.

There are vegetable substitutes for cream and cheese; try until you find any which satisfies you. In some recipes, you can try mashed potatoes as a substitute for cheese, for example, by hydrating the purée with organic milk.

You can make "pâté" by spicing mashed potatoes or hummus, for example.

Remember that almost all the sauces with some animal product have their vegan version, for instance, by replacing regular milk with soy milk.

What about grilled zucchini with a mixture of grounded peppers, garlic and oil? Sautéed mushrooms? Boiled cauliflower served with fried free-range egg, or battered? Boiled Romanesco, with stir-fry garlic and paprika?

Dark chocolate contains no milk, and it is healthier.

Surf the internet for recipes, there are thousands of them. Some of them won't even work for you (those of the book "Ethicarian Cooking" are all proven), but you'll get ideas.

THE STORY OF PROTEINS…

OR

THE COUNT OF PROTEINS.

Proteins are built from amino acids, and there are nine of them which our organism cannot produce by itself and we must consume directly… that is why they are called essential amino acids. They are: histidine, isoleucine, leucine, lysine, methionine, phenylalanine, threonine, tryptophan and valine.

The body needs those amino acids, but they do not need to be consumed simultaneously, as the liver can store them. It is enough to supplement amino acids during the day.

Protein needs are approximately 0.8 per kilogram of weight per day. Thus, a person weighting 70 Kg should consume about 56 grams of protein per day.

Protein metabolism and so on is big enough for a nutrition book, but I think the data we are discussing is enough to understand what we need.

Meat, fish, eggs and milk have all the essential amino acids; vegetables, however: *in many cases each vegetable is individually deficient in certain amino acids.*

Nevertheless, that propaganda saying that animal products meet our protein needs by themselves; although it is true, it forgets to recall that the excess of protein is also harmful, or that a diet based on animal products will fill you with harmful substances, such as cholesterol and it will deprive us of other beneficial ones which we must look for in vegetables.

A totally vegetable diet meets all our needs; the key is in variety and balance. No one is going to feed only on carrots, no matter how vegetarian he/she is, and, if the vegetable diet is varied, he/she won't even have to worry about counting proteins, because the combinations to supplement essential amino acids are as simple as, for instance, cereals with legumes… or not even that, as we can appreciate when seeing the contents of amino acids in some vegetables.

In the diets based on vegetables, due to the deficiencies of certain types of amino acids depending on the plants, an intake of 1 gram of protein per kilogram of weight per day is usually recommended… and let's forget the issue.

As expressed this way it may sound more complicated than it is, we are going to see some examples, in milligrams of amino acid per 100 grams of product, to get an idea and be able to compare:

SOYA

Aspartic acid 3990. Leucine 2840. Glutamic acid 6490. Lysine 1900. Alanine 1530. Methionine 580. Arginine 2360. Proline 1820. Cystine 590. Serine 1690. Phenylalanine 1970. Tyrosine 1250. Glycine 1420. Threonine 1490. Hydroxyproline 0. Tryptophan 450. Histidine 830. Valine 1760. Isoleucine 1780.

CHICKPEAS

Aspartic acid 2444. Leucine 1572. Glutamic acid 3634. Lysine 1479. Alanine 891. Methionine 280. Arginine 1598. Proline 858. Cystine 302. Serine 1076. Phenylalanine 1036. Tyrosine 710. Glycine 864. Threonine 753. Hydroxyproline 0. Tryptophan 172. Histidine 570. Valine 1058. Isoleucine 1231.

WHEAT (flour)

Aspartic acid 398. Leucine 702. Glutamic acid 3318. Lysine 191. Alanine 303. Methionine 147. Arginine 347. Proline 1221. Cystine 208. Serine 502. Phenylalanine 467. Tyrosine 286. Glycine 398. Threonine 277. Hydroxyproline 0. Tryptophan 104. Histidine 181. Valine 416. Isoleucine 372.

RICE

Aspartic acid 657. Leucine 556. Glutamic acid 1330. Lysine 244. Alanine 421. Methionine 143. Arginine 480. Proline 354. Cystine 93. Serine 345. Phenylalanine 328. Tyrosine 219. Glycine 345. Threonine 236. Hydroxyproline 0. Tryptophan 76. Histidine 143. Valine 412. Isoleucine 286.

POTATO

Aspartic acid 430. Leucine 140. Glutamic acid 460. Lysine 130. Alanine 110. Methionine 30. Arginine 120. Proline 110. Cystine 20. Serine 100. Phenylalanine 100. Tyrosine 80. Glycine 120. Threonine 90. Hydroxyproline 0. Tryptophan 30. Histidine 40. Valine 130. Isoleucine 100.

TOMATO

Aspartic acid 113. Leucine 28. Glutamic acid 314. Lysine 27. Alanine 24. Methionine 7. Arginine 17. Proline 15. Cystine 0.93. Serine 26. Phenylalanine 22. Tyrosine 11. Glycine 17. Threonine 21. Hydroxyproline 0. Tryptophan 6. Histidine 12. Valine 21. Isoleucine 21.

ALMOND

Aspartic acid 2158. Leucine 1238. Glutamic acid 4083. Lysine 492. Alanine 789. Methionine 229. Arginine 2332. Proline 764.

Cystine 322. Serine 794. Phenylalanine 984. Tyrosine 526. Glycine 1158. Threonine 517. Hydroxyproline 0. Tryptophan 144. Histidine 441. Valine 967. Isoleucine 746.

EGG

Aspartic acid 1239. Leucine 1069. Glutamic acid 1536. Lysine 755. Alanine 755. Methionine 382. Arginine 755. Proline 500. Cystine 263. Serine 976. Phenylalanine 679. Tyrosine 501. Glycine 450. Threonine 602. Hydroxyproline 0. Tryptophan 195. Histidine 280. Valine 950. Isoleucine 789.

(Whole cow's) MILK

Aspartic acid 230. Leucine 286. Glutamic acid 628. Lysine 222. Alanine 103. Methionine 71. Arginine 103. Proline 270. Cystine 22. Serine 167. Phenylalanine 143. Tyrosine 143. Glycine 61. Threonine 127. Hydroxyproline 0. Tryptophan 39. Histidine 76. Valine 191. Isoleucine 175.

CHICKEN

Aspartic acid 1957. Leucine 1534. Glutamic acid 3181. Lysine 1759. Alanine 1241. Methionine 551. Arginine 1198. Proline 905. Cystine 258. Serine 793. Phenylalanine 784. Tyrosine 655. Glycine 1207. Threonine 870. Hydroxyproline 0. Tryptophan 241. Histidine 523. Valine 1017. Isoleucine 1112.

PORK

Aspartic acid 1664. Leucine 1321. Glutamic acid 2676. Lysine 1509. Alanine 1055. Methionine 488. Arginine 1046. Proline 823. Cystine 205. Serine 763. Phenylalanine 669. Tyrosine 712. Glycine 977. Threonine 857. Hydroxyproline 0. Tryptophan 205. Histidine 677. Valine 977. Isoleucine 866.

Comparative tables regarding the content of essential amino acids per 100 grams of product, in grams:

ESSENTIAL AMINO ACID	CHICKPEA	WHEAT	RICE	POTATO	TOMATO
Histidine	0.57	0.18	0.14	0.04	0.01
Isoleucine	1.23	0.37	0.29	0.10	0.02
Leucine	1.57	0.70	0.56	0.14	0.03
Lysine	1.48	0.19	0.24	0.13	0.03
Methionine	0.28	0.15	0.14	0.03	0.01
Phenylalanine	1.04	0.47	0.33	0.10	0.02
Threonine	0.75	0.28	0.24	0.09	0.02
Tryptophan	0.17	0.10	0.08	0.03	0.01
Valine	1.06	0.42	0.41	0.13	0.02

ESSENTIAL AMINO ACID	ALMOND	EGG	MILK	CHICKEN	PORK	SOYA
Histidine	0.44	0.28	0.08	0.52	0.68	0.83
Isoleucine	0.75	0.79	0.17	1.11	0.87	1.78
Leucine	1.24	1.07	0.29	1.53	1.32	2.84
Lysine	0.49	0.75	0.22	1.76	1.51	1.90
Methionine	0.23	0.38	0.07	0.55	0.49	0.58
Phenylalanine	0.98	0.68	0.14	0.78	0.67	1.97
Threonine	0.52	0.60	0.13	0.87	0.86	1.49
Tryptophan	0.14	0.19	0.04	0.24	0.20	0.45
Valine	0.97	0.95	0.19	1.02	0.98	1.76

Although with words they want us to believe other things, the information in numbers does not lie. It has been proven that vegetables do not have to envy animals, not even regarding proteins, which is what is questioned most.

In eticariana.com.es you will find additional content.

Completed on 2 October 2017,

in Folgoso de la Ribera (Spain).

Dedicated to the animals, those martyrs....

and to the people who fight for them.

www.ingramcontent.com/pod-product-compliance
Lightning Source LLC
Chambersburg PA
CBHW060757260726
48660CB00002B/670